PRESTON BUSES BEFORE AND AFTER DEREGULATION

Mike Rhodes

First published 2019

Amberley Publishing
The Hill, Stroud
Gloucestershire, GL5 4EP

www.amberley-books.com

Copyright © Mike Rhodes, 2019

The right of Mike Rhodes to be identified as the Author of this work has been asserted in accordance with the Copyrights, Designs and Patents Act 1988.

ISBN 978 1 4456 8378 2 (print)
ISBN 978 1 4456 8379 9 (ebook)

All rights reserved. No part of this book may be reprinted or reproduced or utilised in any form or by any electronic, mechanical or other means, now known or hereafter invented, including photocopying and recording, or in any information storage or retrieval system, without the permission in writing from the Publishers.

British Library Cataloguing in Publication Data.
A catalogue record for this book is available from the British Library.

Orgination by Amberley Publishing.
Printed in the UK.

Introduction

The first registered public transport service in Preston was a horse-drawn tram route, which was operated by the Preston Tramways Company and commenced running to Fulwood on 20 March 1879. Additional services soon commenced to Ashton, Broadgate and Farringdon Park. By 1886 these had been leased to a company by the name of Hardings and the tram depot was situated on Fishergate Hill, adjacent to the main London to Scotland railway line. Harding's lease expired on 31 December 1903 and the Corporation had applied for consent to construct its own electric tramways in 1900 and 1902. Consequently, electric tram services commenced, running to Fulwood Barracks via North Road and Farringdon Park on 7 June 1904. Twenty-six open-top four-wheel tramcars and four bogie cars were purchased from the town's Electric Railway & Tramway Carriage Works, which was situated in Strand Road. Additional services soon followed running to Ashton, Penwortham (Broadgate), Fulwood via Deepdale and Ribbleton. At its maximum (between 1920 and 1926) the Corporation operated a total of forty-eight tramcars from its purpose-built depot in Deepdale Road. The depot was enlarged with a new administrative office block in 1915 to cater for an expanding fleet.

The first buses purchased were three Leyland G7s for a service to Lytham Road, which began running on 23 January 1922. It was originally hoped to construct a tramway along Adelphi Street and Plungington Road, but the conditions imposed to widen these thoroughfares proved insurmountable and the service was consequently provided using motorbuses. Further bus routes to Ashton Lane Ends and Frenchwood commenced running in June 1924, for which additional vehicles were procured. By 1930 there were sixteen single-deck and five double-deck buses in the fleet, and the majority of these were housed in a small garage that had been constructed on the opposite side of Holmrook Road, facing the tram depot. The first double-deck buses entered the fleet in 1926, and consisted of three Leyland Leviathans, which were employed on the Plungington Road service. In 1931 the town council voted to replace all of the trams with motorbuses, and consequently a new bus garage was constructed on the side of the tram depot, which necessitated the closure of a section of Holmrook Road. Opened in 1932, the new facilities also included a small maintenance area that could accommodate five buses. Between 1931 and 1938 the Corporation purchased seventy-three new buses, which replaced the trams and all of the early buses other than the four 1929 Leyland Lions.

Prior to the Second World War, the Lytham Road service was extended to Queens Drive and further bus routes were started to Holme Slack and Moorside, while post-war new housing estates were served at Brookfield, Ingol, Larches, Lea, Moor Nook (Moorside) and Ribbleton. To cater for the post-war expansion, thirty-one PD1s were purchased in 1946/47, which increased the fleet size to 103 vehicles. Throughout the 1950s the pre-war Titans were replaced by successive batches of PD2s. The first 30-foot-long and also the first 8-foot-wide buses entered service in January 1959 in the form of a batch of seven PD3/4s. These were followed by three more batches of PD3s. Between 1959 and 1967, the Corporation embarked on an ambitious programme of rebuilding a number of PD2s into the larger PD3 configuration. There had always been a need to operate low-height vehicles on the Ashton service, which passed under the height- and width-restricted Fylde Road Railway Bridge, even during the days of tramway operation. However, in 1957 the road was lowered under the bridge, thus eliminating this requirement. Not only were the four low-height PD2s rebuilt, but an additional four of the highbridge buses were also treated. The resultant vehicles had an increased seating capacity of fifteen and twelve respectively. The depot was further enlarged in 1964 to accommodate buses that until then had been parked out in the open yard, while two years later the fleet colours were radically changed from maroon and cream to blue and ivory.

In July 1968 the government introduced a grant that was available to bus operators who purchased buses that were suitable for one-person operation. This had a dramatic effect on the bus industry as manufactures developed new bus designs that conformed to the government's requirements. This spawned a number of varieties of new single-deckers, most of which incorporated two sets of doors. Looking to reduce costs, the Transport Committee elected to implement a programme of converting routes to operation with one-person operated buses and duly ordered two batches of Leyland's new Panther range, five of which were bodied by Metro-Cammell Weymann and ten by Marshall's of Cambridge. The Panther fleet reached its peak in 1972, with a total of forty-one of the type in service. The undertaking had remained loyal to the Leyland plant for sixty-four years, buying nothing but Leyland chassis, other than in 1976, when a small batch of three Bristol LHS midibuses joined the fleet to work new estate routes. Except for these three, all of the buses that entered the fleet up until 1986 were of Leyland manufacture, as the Panthers were followed by several batches of Atlanteans between 1974 and 1983.

The size of the fleet had remained fairly constant from 1947 until 1979, only fluctuating over the intervening years between a low of ninety-one in 1971 and a high of 102 in 1958. This pictorial account covers a fourteen-year period in the history of the operator and starts with the year 1979 when the fleet size stood at ninety-six and comprised forty Atlanteans, forty-one Panthers, three Bristol midibuses and twelve PD3s. The photographs have been arranged in chronological order and have been chosen to illustrate the various changes to the fleet and expansion and alterations to the route network over a seven-year period, either side of deregulation. The illustrations have been deliberately chosen to depict as much of the operating area as possible, and to this end the number of views that show the bus station and its environs have been kept to a minimum.

The period covered by the book features the withdrawal of the last of the front-engined buses in the fleet followed by the gradual replacement of the Panthers with more Atlanteans and the subsequent replacement of the first batches of Atlanteans with Olympians and Lynxes. Though the fleet size dipped to a pre-war minimum of eighty-three in 1984/85, this was only a prelude to the significant expansion that followed deregulation in 1986. The following year Preston Bus faced what would then be the most challenging period in its history when United Transport (trading as Zippy) introduced a comprehensive network of town minibus services between April and July 1987. This sparked an intensive tit-for-tat period as each operator strove to keep ahead of its competitors. New areas of bus operation were opened up as routes were devised to penetrate the various housing estates, made possible by the use of the much smaller minibuses. These were operated at very frequent intervals, with just five-minute headways in some instances, and also employed the principle of 'hail and ride', which did not require the installation of bus stops at specific stopping places.

In March 1988 United Transport was bought out by Ribble, who continued to operate much the same level of services. Consequently, Preston Bus introduced a number of minibus routes that ventured beyond the town boundaries. Competition remained intense between the two operators until Ribble was acquired by Stagecoach in April 1989. Later that year common sense eventually prevailed and each operator made significant changes and concentrated on their original areas of operation. At its peak, Preston Bus, as the undertaking had become known, operated a fleet of fifty-two minibuses (four more second-hand examples were acquired in 1991 specifically for use on the Part Way Park & Ride service), and at the close of 1989 the fleet size stood at 130 vehicles. Between 1989 and 1992 new bus acquisitions were concentrated on replacing the Atlantean fleet. While six of the first batch of Alexanders had passed to North Western in 1987, a further thirty-four Atlanteans were disposed of during this period and were replaced by a mixture of Lynx and Olympians.

In the year 1179, King Henry II conferred upon the burgesses of the town a royal charter, which gave them the right to hold a 'Guild Merchant'. However, it was not until 1542 that this right was enacted on a regular basis, at intervals of once every twenty years. This continued until 1922, with the following Guild being moved to 1952 on account of the Second World War. It followed then that a Preston Guild was held in 1992, and as in previous Guilds the various local bus operators had a big part to play. Several large processions would be held during Guild Week (the first week in September), which were watched by tens of thousands of people, all of whom descended on the town in a relatively short period of time. All available vehicles would be pressed into service at these times. In addition, there would be many special duties to cater for, such as additional Park & Ride services and the transportation of school children to event venues. The 1992 Guild was no different and a visit to the depot on the afternoon of 3 September revealed just four buses that were not on the road.

Pictures of Atlanteans tend to dominate this review, but this was their zenith period, during which time the fleet was largely made up of the type. This account ends in 1993 when the undertaking was sold to a management and employee consortium. The next chapter would see the first generation of minibuses replaced by more suitable vehicles, and several years in the future would be the infamous period of bus wars between Preston Bus and Stagecoach.

I hope the reader enjoys the illustrations and gains some knowledge of Preston's local bus operations over this interesting period.

Mike Rhodes
January 2019

The Corporation's trams and buses were painted maroon and cream from the outset. The first buses to carry the predominantly maroon layout were Leyland Leviathans Nos 63/4 in 1926. The layout seen here on Metro-Cammell-bodied Leyland PD3A/1 No. 72 was introduced in 1956 with the delivery of the first batch of Crossley-bodied Leyland PD2/10s. No. 72 is seen parked outside the Transport Offices in Lancaster Road, *c.* 1967.

In the autumn of 1966, livery experiments were carried out using four Leyland PD2s, and a new livery of mid-blue and ivory was adopted, as seen on 1961 Metro-Cammell-bodied Leyland PD3/4 No. 18. The last maroon painted buses were replaced by new Leyland Panthers in 1970. No. 18 is seen at the junction of Church Street and Stanley Street before the ring road was constructed, returning from Ribbleton Gamull Lane.

In November 1973 the livery arrangement was changed again, with the buses being predominantly painted ivory. The Ashton Lane Ends C route was converted to 'PAYB' operation on 1 December 1972 but remained crew-worked on Sundays only until 5 September 1976. 1965-built Metro-Cammell-bodied Leyland PD3A/1 No. 73 is seen in Eldon Street on 22 August 1976 and will next work through from the bus station to Holme Slack.

The jointly operated P4 service to Ingol commenced running on 13 February 1965, but it would be several years before the route was established as a primary service. It was converted to PAYB operation in October 1976, but certain journeys continued to be operated by crewed buses, as evidenced by Metro-Cammell-bodied Leyland PD3A/1 No. 87, which is seen standing at the Barry Avenue terminus on 6 May 1977.

Preston Corporation became well known for its PD3 Rebuilds. No. 5 was new in March 1952 as a fifty-five-seat lowbridge PD2/10. It was rebuilt in 1960 as a seventy-seat PD3/6. It is seen passing the parish church in Church Street on 7 July 1977 while working on the jointly operated (with Ribble Motors) P5 service from Ribbleton to Hutton.

You will have to take the author's word regarding this picture. It is highbridge PD3/6 Rebuild No. 59 departing the bus station in a snow storm on 10 April 1978 on the PL service to Queens Drive. No. 59 was the last of the eight Rebuilds and entered service in September 1967. It survived until October 1978 but had been scrapped by the mid-1980s.

The majority of the post-war Leyland Titans in the Preston fleet met an ignominious end and were snapped up by scrap merchants. No. 62 was one of a batch of seven Metro-Cammell-bodied Leyland PD3/5s that were new in December 1958. No. 62 was withdrawn in May 1978 and was sold to Geoff Lister at Bolton before moving on to C. F. Booth's scrap yard at Rotherham. It awaits its fate at Deepdale with two others of the batch on 25 May 1978.

In January 1976, 1954-built Leyland PD2/10s Nos 54/7 were converted to permanent driver training buses, replacing similar bus No. 43 and PD2/1 No. 125. While No. 57 retained its fleet number, No. 54 was renumbered to TU1. It is seen here performing training duties in Tulketh Brow. The two PD2/10s were replaced by two converted PD3/4s in 1980.

The jointly operated P2 service from Penwortham to Fulwood commenced running on 1 January 1948. It was exclusively operated by Ribble Motors and was converted to 'PAYB' operation on 4 April 1970 using dual-door Bristol RELLs. The service was extended a short distance to the west side of the West Coast Main Line (WCML) in November 1977 and from 17 April 1978 the operation passed to Borough of Preston and reverted to crew operation. 1963-built Metro-Cammell-bodied Leyland PD3A/1 No. 90 is seen at Lightfoot Lane on 6 January 1979.

Snow of any significance is somewhat of a rarity in Preston. However, January 1979 proved the exception. Preston's first Atlanteans had been a batch of ten bodied by Walter Alexander, which were received in late 1974/early 1975. No. 105 is seen in Black Bull Lane on 27 January 1979, returning to town. It was to be many more years before buses showed 'Bus Station' when heading back to town.

The 'Cross Town Service' commenced running between the Cemetery and Haslam Park at Ashton on 19 September 1932. It was withdrawn during the war years and was reinstated as a very limited 'Works Service' from Lane Ends in June 1948. Later using the letters LEC (98 from November 1980), it continued in operation until 31 December 1999. 1961-built Metro-Cammell-bodied Leyland PD3/4 No. 15 is seen crossing the WCML in Eldon Street on 24 May 1979 with the solitary 07.29 Monday to Friday journey from Lane Ends.

Leyland Vehicles produced their first two prototype Titans in 1975. Development was slow, and it wasn't until June 1977 that a third demonstrator took to the roads. This was BCK 706R, which was on loan to Preston BT for two weeks in June 1979. It is seen in St George's Road on 15 June, returning from Holme Slack. It was somewhat over-engineered for the provincial market and consequently the vast majority of the type were ordered by London Transport.

The Ashton Lane Ends C service commenced running on 13 November 1936. It was linked across town with the Holme Slack service until it was converted to 'PAYB' operation using Leyland Panthers on 1 December 1972 (Sundays excepted). A combination of longer buses and parked cars often caused access difficulties at the Ashton terminus. East Lancashire Coachbuilders (ELC)-bodied Leyland Atlantean No. 119 and Metro-Cammell-bodied Leyland Panther No. 203 have been held up in Stocks Road on 11 August 1979.

In September 1979, Blackpool Transport experienced a shortage of serviceable buses. Seddon-bodied Leyland Panthers Nos 230/2 were loaned to Blackpool from 5 to 16 September, at which point they were replaced by Nos 233/4 until the 27th. No. 234 is seen inside the Rigby Road garage on 21 September 1979. A number of Blackpool AEC Swifts can be seen parked in the background.

All-over advert buses in the Preston fleet were somewhat of a rarity until ELC-bodied Atlantean No. 115 received this Matthew Brown advert in 1979. It is seen in Watling Street Road on 23 September, just a few days after being painted. Despite the destination, the bus is returning to town from Fulwood Row.

Buses were first provided to the Continuation Hospital in Longsands Lane from Sunday 16 December 1951 with the extension of certain journeys on the FR service. A dedicated service commenced on 17 May 1954 with a single journey on Wednesday and Saturday afternoons and Thursday and Sunday evenings. The Sunday service was altered to run in the afternoon sometime in 1973, and Metro-Cammell-bodied Leyland PD3/4 No. 14 is seen in Midgery Lane on 23 September 1979, waiting for the return departure to town at 15.40.

Having first commenced a service to Frenchwood in June 1924, it was extended to Lower Frenchwood in December 1928 using the letters FR. From 1 January 1948 it became the jointly operated P1, with buses running through to Lea (and later Larches Estate). 1968-built Marshall-bodied Panther No. 215 is seen in Ashworth Grove on 31 December 1979, having worked through from Larches (the Lea journeys were renumbered to P3 in February 1965).

For many years the FP service was linked with the PL Queens Drive/Boys Lane services. However, following the conversion of the PL to 'PAYB' operation in August 1978, the FP was henceforth linked with the HS. 1961-built Metro-Cammell-bodied Leyland PD3/4 No. 19 has just turned into Harewood Road when seen on its return journey from Holme Slack on 2 January 1980.

Also working on the HS/FP services just a couple of weeks later, on 26 January, is Metro-Cammell-bodied Leyland PD3A/1 No. 85, one of a batch of seven that replaced an equal number of PD1s in November 1963. The remaining PD3s were in their last few weeks of operation at this time.

Operation of front-engined PD3s virtually came to an end on 21 March 1980 when the remaining examples, other than Nos 69 and 70, were withdrawn from service. On 17 February 1980, Nos 14/5 were used for a commemorative tour, while No. 13 was used on the afternoon trip to the Continuation Hospital. Nos 13/4 are seen together in Longsands Lane, opposite the hospital.

Preston Buses Before and After Deregulation 17

With only a few weeks to go before withdrawal, 1963-built Metro-Cammell-bodied Leyland PD3A/1 No. 90 approaches journey's end on the FP service and is seen in Cairnsmore Avenue on 1 March 1980. The FP/16 has run continuously to Farringdon Park since 7 June 1904 and was still going strong in 2018.

As previously mentioned, PD3 operation virtually ended during the third week in March 1980 when Nos 13/4, 71/2/3, and 90 were all withdrawn. Their replacements were a batch of ten Leyland Atlanteans with bodywork by Walter Alexander of Falkirk. Nos 145/3/2/4 are seen in the dock shop on 2 March 1980, prior to entering service.

With only five days to go before withdrawal, 1961-built Metro-Cammell-bodied Leyland PD3/4 No. 13 is seen in Strand Road on 16 March 1980, having performed a Works Special from the bus station. The world-famous GEC (formerly English Electric, and prior to that, Dick, Kerr factory) can be seen in the background. In the 1950s and early 1960s this complex used to generate a multitude of 'Works' buses.

Preston operated a total of forty-one Leyland Panthers with bodywork variously supplied by Marshalls, Metro-Cammell Weymann and Seddon. The Ashton A 'Main' bus service commenced running on 6 August 1934 (there was also a separate A service from Corporation Street at this time) and replaced the original tram service, which dated back to 30 June 1904. It was converted to 'PAYB' operation on 6 May 1971 (Sundays excepted) using Leyland Panthers. 1970-built Marshall-bodied example No. 218 is seen in Tulketh Road, heading for town, on 23 August 1980.

Football specials to Preston North End's Deepdale stadium have run since the early days of the trams and are still operated in 2018. On occasion buses have been provided to transfer 'visiting' supporters between the railway station and the ground. For the visit of West Ham United on 23 August 1980, Alexander-bodied Atlanteans Nos 106/9/10 performed this duty. The match ended in a 0-0 draw.

The Alexander AL bodies on the 1980-built Atlateans were a stylish design that didn't look out of place in 2018. The destination apertures were set lower than on Nos 101–10, which made them instantly recognisable. Looking as though it has just come out of the box, No. 148 is seen in Watling Street Road on 24 August 1980, returning to town from Fulwood Row.

The first services converted to 'PAYB' operation commenced on 2 December 1968 using fifteen new dual-door Leyland Panthers, the first five of which were bodied by Metro-Cammell Weymann. The first Panther to be withdrawn was No. 202 on 8 September 1980. Seen just two days earlier in Lancaster Road is sister vehicle No. 203. Services commenced running to the post-war Moor Nook estate on 8 March 1952.

For many years the A, C and PL services were routed out of town via Fishergate and Lune Street. Following the construction of the ring road they were altered to use Fox Street from March 1968. They frequently encountered heavy traffic and severe delays, and consequently they were altered to use a contra-flow bus lane on Friargate from 1 May 1972. Seddon-bodied Panther No. 228 is followed by Marshall-bodied No. 209 on the C and Alexander-bodied Atlantean No. 141 on the PL as they load outside St George's Shopping Centre on 1 November 1980.

Sunday 2 November 1980 was the last day that the bus services were denoted by pneumonics (letters). 1971-built Seddon-bodied Panther No. 227 is seen turning from Blackpool Road into Waterloo Road on the jointly operated P3, which ran through to Frenchwood. From the following day the two services were split, with the P3 (Lea) becoming the 26 and the P3 (Frenchwood) becoming the 29, while the interworked P1 to Larches became the 27.

Also seen on the last day is 1968 Marshall-bodied Panther No. 213, which is negotiating the Adelphi roundabout on the Ashton Lane Ends C. All of the Panthers and Atlanteans (except the last two) were built with two doors, which was the nationwide trend at the time for new 'PAYB'-equipped buses.

The third and final picture that has been included of operations on 2 November 1980 depicts 1979-built ELC-bodied Atlantean No. 140 at the Lane Ends terminus. Not only was this the last day for route letters, but it was also the last day of operation of the C. No more would buses stand at the Kimberley Road stop as from the following day the C was replaced by service 33, which ran beyond Lane Ends to Tanterton.

Monday 3 November 1980 saw buses displaying route numbers for the first time. 1980-built Alexander-bodied Atlantean No. 142 is seen on Fishergate Bridge on the 27 (previously the P1), while going towards town is Seddon-bodied Panther No. 224 on service 21 (BR) from Broadgate.

This view taken near the entrance to No. 4 garage (opened in 1964) on 22 February 1981 depicts 1975-built Alexander-bodied Atlantean No. 104 and on-loan Leyland Titan demonstrator NHG 732P. The lower section of the front end of No. 104 was modified following an accident in January 1980, with five more of the batch also receiving the same treatment over a number of years. The Titan later passed to J. Fishwick & Sons of nearby Leyland.

Among all the Panthers and Atlanteans, the Undertaking also operated three Duple-bodied Bristol LHS midibuses. These had been purchased in May 1976 to operate three estate routes: the CL, G and P7. The CL to Callon was short-lived and only ran for eleven months, but the other two services continued until deregulation in 1986. There was generally one spare bus and No. 342 is seen being employed on the 99 (not the 7), which ran between the Royal Preston Hospital and Moor Nook, on 25 March 1981.

Two of the original tram services that commenced running in June 1904 were the D (Deepdale) and the F (Fulwood), which were generally referred to as the Inner and Outer Circle routes. The services remained unaltered for decades and became the 15 and 20 upon the adoption of route numbers. 1971-built Seddon-bodied Panther No. 229 is seen in Watling Street Road on 17 April 1981 on the Outer Circle 20.

Service 99 was introduced in March 1981 and was a limited service that was intended to provide transport for hospital workers from the east side of the town. Any type of bus in the fleet could turn up on these workings and the pristine 1972-built Seddon-bodied Panther No. 235 is seen waiting time inside the hospital grounds on 16 May 1981.

Preston Buses Before and After Deregulation

Buses first commenced running to Longsands on 30 May 1938 when a few journeys on the GL were extended from Gamull Lane and it only ever comprised a handful of daily journeys. In November 1980, the Brookfield BF, Fulwood Row FR and Longsands LS services all adopted the same route number, 36. Alexander-bodied Atlantean No. 145 is seen in Longsands Lane on 24 May 1981 with the lunchtime departure to town. This locality has since changed beyond recognition.

Following the withdrawal of the majority of the PD3s in March 1980, Nos 69 and 70 continued in service for a good while longer. No. 70 is seen descending Church Street on 29 June 1981 on the additional crew-operated 07.20 (M–F) to Brookfield. It is unable to display the correct route number, 36.

The HS service to Holme Slack commenced running on 17 February 1936 and for many years it was linked across town to the Ashton C. While through running to Ashton ceased in December 1972, it was later linked with the FP until conversion to 'PAYB' operation on 14 January 1980. 1976-built ELC-bodied Atlantean No. 117 is seen in Harewood Road under a threatening sky on 2 July 1981 on what has now become service 14.

The Ashton Lane Ends to Cemetery service was routed via a myriad of back roads rather than the direct arterial road (Blackpool Road). Alexander-bodied Atlantean No. 105 is seen in the parallel (to Harewood Road) St Stephen's Road on 2 July 1981 with the 07.29 solitary journey from Ashton Lane Ends to the Cemetery. At this time there were three early morning journeys in the opposite direction.

Metro-Cammell-bodied Leyland PD3A/1 No. 69 had been new in April 1965 and was finally retired on 16 July 1981. Just one week before its withdrawal it is seen outside the GEC factory in Strand Road, waiting to depart for the bus station via Fylde Road at 12.36. While the east works on the opposite side of the road was demolished in 1990, the building behind the bus was owned by Alstom in 2018, although the works were earmarked for closure later that year, ending over 120 years of road and rail transport technology on this site.

The operator was called upon on a number of occasions to provide buses for special occasions. On 2 September 1981, ten buses were used for a BAe (British Aerospace) private hire from Preston to Chester. Nine of the vehicles provided were Panthers, and Nos 231 and 239 are seen in St Martin's Way, heading for the city's Roodee coach park. The other vehicles involved were Nos 232/3/5/6/7/40/1 and on-loan Leopard coach VCW 85V.

By the end of 1981 there were sixty-five Atlanteans in the fleet. They had replaced the last of the PD2s, all of the PD3s and were now making inroads into the Panthers. ELC-bodied No. 121 entered service on 14 October 1977. It is seen nearly four years later, on 6 September 1981, turning around at the Broadgate terminus. This location was one of the original tram termini, which dated back to 1904.

The last of the PD3 Titans, No. 70, finally bowed out on 1 November 1981. It was used by a group of enthusiasts to tour the route system and beyond. Its final duty was on the afternoon return trip to the Continuation Hospital. It is seen in Windy Street in the village of Chipping, some 10 miles to the east of Preston. It was sold to Passenger Vehicle Spares (PVS) at Barnsley and was then broken up by Carlton Metals.

In November 1980 the PL service became the 22. The PL was the first Corporation service to be operated by buses and had commenced operation on 23 January 1922. The original terminus had been at Lytham Road. The route was successively extended to Boys Lane, then Queens Drive and then to Sharoe Green Lane by the date of this picture, 12 December 1981. It was converted to 'PAYB' operation on 7 August 1978 at the same time as the latter extension. Atlantean No. 123 waits to depart back to town while No. 132 approaches the terminus.

The winter of 1980/81 was probably Preston's harshest winter since that of 1962/63, which gripped the whole country. Fairly new ELC-bodied Atlantean No. 152 is seen on Fishergate Bridge on 14 December 1981, returning to town. The Broadgate was a relatively short route, with around ten minutes being allowed for each direction of travel.

At the time of this picture, 19 December 1981, the Holme Slack service was operated by a mixture of Panthers and Atlanteans. 1972 Seddon-bodied Panther No. 231 is about to turn out of St Gregory Road into Skeffington Road. As previously mentioned the ultimate destination would be shown throughout the round trip and the bus is actually returning to town.

The snowy conditions persisted throughout most of December. Prior to November 1980 the principal service to Lea had been the P3, which operated via Waterloo Road. This was then downgraded to a limited service, which was given the service number 26. At the same time a new service commenced running to Lea via Garstang Road, which also took the number 26. Alexander-bodied Atlantean No. 143 is seen alongside Moor Park in Garstang Road on 19 December 1981.

The building that currently houses the dock shop was constructed in 1904 and was the original tram shed. Following the demise of the trams in 1935, the rails and tramway pits were removed and it continued in use as a bus garage. It was internally redesigned and fitted out with inspection pits in 1965. Seen over the pits on 17 January 1982 are Bristol LHS No. 344 and Atlanteans Nos 101/46. Although the buses have changed, the layout was still exactly the same in 2018.

It is Sunday 7 February 1982 and a number of Seddon Pennine-bodied Panthers are lined up inside No. 2 garage ready for their Monday morning duties. At this time there were still twenty Panthers in the fleet, though by the end of the year a further seven would have been withdrawn.

1971-built Seddon-bodied Panther No. 227 is seen in Ribbleton Avenue on 26 March 1982, working from Moor Nook to the Royal Preston Hospital at Fulwood. No. 227 was withdrawn later that year, while service 99 continued to operate until 29 July 2007.

A pile of smouldering timber is all that is left of a row of terraced houses and shops following their demolition. 1981-built ELC-bodied Atlantean No. 151 is proceeding down Water Lane on 26 March 1982. Service 24 had been the Ashton A service. The buildings were demolished to make way for road improvement works. The blue brick arch bridge carries the Preston to Blackpool railway line over the road and was in the process of being electrified as these notes were being prepared.

The batch of Atlanteans numbered 158–65 entered service in November/December 1981 and continued the trend of replacing forty-eight-seat single-deckers with eighty-two-seat double-deckers. No. 161 is seen in Fulwood Row on 12 April 1982, returning from Longsands Lane. The terminus of this route was variously referred to as Long Sand Lane, Longsands and Longsands Lane over the years. It ceased to operate after 12 July 1987.

ELC-bodied Atlantean No. 157 passes between The Wheatsheaf and The Grand Junction public houses (both of which were still going strong in 2018) at the foot of Tulketh Road on 9 May 1982. Services 24 and 26 were both withdrawn in June 1984 and replaced by a new service, numbered 25, which operated via the 24 route to Pedders Lane and then continued via the 26 route to Lea.

On 31 May 1982, Pope John Paul II celebrated mass at Heaton Park in Manchester, and the huge congregation was drawn from the surrounding populous. Eight Preston Atlanteans, Nos 158–65, were among the hundreds of buses used to transport the pilgrims. Nos 161/4 are seen parked on a newly constructed stretch of the M66 (now part of the M60) at Simister, which was used to park up the buses before it was officially opened to the general motoring fraternity.

As vehicle disposals go, there can't have been any more unusual than the circumstances surrounding Panther No. 228. Still in service on 17 June 1982, it was withdrawn following an enquiry for a surplus vehicle. Since all the previously withdrawn buses had been sold, No. 228 was taken out of service and the following day it was taken to a yard in Bamber Bridge. It is seen having its paint stripped on 20 June prior to its conversion to a mobile video library.

The last route to employ conductors was the 16, which was converted to 'PAYB' operation from 22 March 1982. Alexander-bodied Atlantean No. 141 is seen in New Hall Lane on 18 September 1982. This bus was loaned to Lothian Regional Transport in April 1981, and following withdrawal in May 2001 it passed into preservation.

The former Stratford Blue/Midland Red Marshall Camair-bodied Panthers were originally numbered 230–4 when they joined the fleet in November 1971. They were renumbered the following year to 237–41, and No. 237 is seen in Deepdale Road (now Sir Tom Finney Way) on 25 September 1982 on the Outer Circle route. They were reseated from B41D to B47D in 1980, following the removal of a rather generous luggage pen.

Service 13, known as the Inner Link, was the brainchild of one of the Transport Committee borough councillors, and it operated on Saturdays only from 9 October 1982 until 8 January 1983. Encircling the town centre, its timing point was in Pedder Street, in the shadow of St Walburge's Church. Duple-bodied Bristol LHS No. 344 is seen passing the Market Square on the first Saturday of operation.

The turning circle at Holme Slack was brought into use on 17 April 1978, prior to which the bus had to perform a reversing manoeuvre at the junction of Holme Slack Lane and Lily Grove (behind the photographer). 1978-built ELC-bodied Atlantean No. 127 is seen in snowy conditions on 12 December 1982, waiting to return to town.

Service 33 had commenced running on 3 November 1980 to a developing area north of the town known as Tanterton. Alexander-bodied Atlantean No. 146 is seen turning out of Tanterton Hall Road into Tag Lane on 31 December 1982. The construction works taking place were for the formation of a new roundabout, which formed a new junction with the then soon to be constructed Tom Benson Way.

Sunday 9 January 1983 sees a deserted Lancaster Road in the town centre. ELC-bodied Atlantean No. 123 is seen heading for Farringdon Park while one-month-old similar vehicle No. 166 is on the Moor Nook service. The imposing building on the left is the Harris Museum & Art Gallery, which houses the town's (city's) central library. It was opened in 1893.

In October 1982, Panther No. 236 was painted with this promotional advert colour scheme for the 'Red Rose Rambler' ticket. The RRR was promoted by Lancashire County Council and was embraced by most of the Lancashire bus operators and the local railway network. The official launch didn't take place until 28 March 1983. No. 236 is seen at the junction of North Road and Moor Lane on 9 January 1983.

Another view taken at the same location on the same day sees Alexander-bodied Atlantean No. 145 on the Inner Circle service 15 (formerly the D). When this bus was retired from service in May 2001, it was converted into a Mobile Learning Centre for Preston College. While the Moorbrook public house was still going strong in 2018, the roundabout junction had been replaced by traffic signals.

The Frenchwood route was the second bus service to be established in the mid-1920s. From 1 January 1948 it had formed part of the jointly operated P1 service to Lea (and Larches). Following the service changes implemented on 3 November 1980, it became a standalone route from town, although for operational purposes it was linked to the Broadgate. Marshall Camair-bodied Panther No. 241 is seen in Ashworth Grove on 19 February 1983.

The midibus routes to Grange (G) and Savick (P7) commenced running on 30 August 1976 and were almost exclusively operated by two of the Bristol LHSs. These became services 12 and 30 and were linked for operational purposes. Dual-purpose-seated No. 342 is seen in Blackpool Road, returning from Grange on 23 February 1983. It will form the next departure to Savick, which has already been displayed on the blind.

Only a handful of Panthers were sold for scrap and the majority saw further service with other operators. Thirteen of the type were bought by the Isle of Man National Transport. No. 225 had been withdrawn by Preston in November 1982 and was sold later that month to the IOMNT, becoming No. 5 in their fleet. It is seen in Douglas bus station on 28 May 1983, along with former Tyne & Wear Alexander-bodied Atlantean No. 66 and 1963 Willowbrook-bodied Leyland PD3A/1 No. 45.

The Transport Department were frequently supportive of local events. On Sunday 19 June 1983 a half marathon event was held in the town, and buses were provided to transport the runners to and from a number of Park & Ride sites to the start/finish point at Moor Park. Seen parked in Deepdale Road (Sir Tom Finney Way), opposite Moor Park, are Atlanteans Nos 143/41/67/06/44/17. In all, sixteen buses were provided for the event.

Alexander-bodied Atlantean No. 106 (with a modified front end) is seen in Deepdale Road, with Preston North End's somewhat dated west stand in the background. This was the first stand to be demolished during the total reconstruction of the ground between 1995 and 2008. Some upcoming matches are shown on the fixtures board, including an international match. The picture is dated 19 June 1983.

The buses were used to operate Park & Ride services from the bus station, market and Avenham car parks to Moor Park. ELC-bodied Atlantean No. 122 has just dropped off a group of race participants in St Thomas' Road on 19 June 1983 when spotted.

Preston Borough Transport (PBT) operated a total of seventy-nine Atlanteans. The final two were delivered in June 1983 as Nos 1 and 2. They differed in a number of ways from the rest, most noticeably in having a single door and being painted in a different livery style. Service 28 had previously been the P2 and it was extended from Fulwood to Tanterton, via Lightfoot Lane, from 13 June 1983. Atlantean No. 1 is seen when virtually brand new working the Tag Lane loop section of the route at Tanterton.

In 1983 the British Golf Open Championship was held at the Royal Birkdale course in Southport. A special bus service was provided from the centre of Southport to the course, which was operated by buses from Merseyside PTE, PBT and Ribble. Virtually brand-new ELC-bodied Atlanteans Nos 175/3/4 are seen loading in the town's Esplanade on 16 July.

The PL/22 service had always been a frequent bus service, with buses running at five to six-minute intervals at certain times of the day. ELC-bodied Atlantean No. 132 picks up passengers outside the Blind Home in Black Bull Lane on 21 January 1984. The origin of the ornate bus shelter has been the subject of some discussion over the years, but it was most likely erected by the erstwhile Fulwood Urban District Council, which was absorbed by Preston Borough Council on 1 April 1974.

An unusual scene sees 1981-built ELC-bodied Atlantean No. 158 working on midibus service 30 to Savick. Originally the jointly operated P7, the service commenced running on 14 October 1974, initially using crew-operated PD2s. Although jointly operated, Ribble never provided any buses for this service. No. 158 is seen in Fylde Road on 18 February 1984 with the infamous restricted railway bridge in the background.

Another of the late 1981 batch of Atlanteans was No. 160, which is seen arriving at the revised terminus for service 20 on 27 April 1984. From 13 June 1983 the Inner and Outer Circulars were altered to conventional out and back routes, with both services being extended from Watling Street Road to the Sharoe Green Lane turning circle. The Harlequin chocolates advert could be seen on buses belonging to a number of bus fleets in the North West around this time.

ELC-bodied Atlantean No. 126 is seen climbing Tulketh Road, also on 27 April 1984. The original service to Ashton commenced running with horse-drawn trams on 23 December 1882. Following the closure of the horse tram system on 31 December 1903, a new electric tram service was inaugurated on 30 June 1904, which was converted to motorbus operation on 6 August 1934.

Following the service changes in November 1980, service 33 served Tanterton via Brook Street and service 34 ran to Ingol via Fylde Road. However, at certain times of the week and all day on Sunday, the 33 was replaced by the 44, which ran to Ingol via Brook Street. Alexander-bodied Atlantean No. 143 is seen in Brook Street on Saturday 28 April 1984, returning to town. On this occasion, the 44 was running in lieu of the 33 due to a road closure on Tulketh Brow.

Over the weekend of 28/29 April 1984, the railway line to Blackpool was closed to permit the replacement of the cast-iron bridge spanning Waterloo Road. The rail replacement service was provided jointly by PBT and Ribble. Atlanteans Nos 176/51 wait at the bottom of Butler Street on 29 April 1984 for their next turn of duty. The period East Lancashire entrance to the station (behind the Ribble buses) was demolished not long afterwards to make way for station improvement works, which were carried out in conjunction with the construction of the Fishergate Shopping Centre.

Following the withdrawal of a number of Panthers in June 1983, the operator retained the remaining three for a further fourteen months. Frequently seen on service 27 during their last months of operation, No. 33 is seen descending Wellfield Road on 7 May 1984. Immaculately turned out as usual, No. 33, along with Nos 35/6 (previously Nos 233/5/6), was finally withdrawn on 28 August and all three went to the IOMNT.

The first Olympian to join the fleet was Eastern Coach Works-bodied No. 3, which first arrived on 23 February 1984. However, it spent virtually all of its first fourteen months operating as a demonstrator for Leyland Bus. It is seen in such a capacity on loan to Blackpool Borough Transport, and is about to depart Talbot Road bus station on 12 May 1984.

Accidents do happen. However, the circumstances surrounding the damage caused to Alexander-bodied Atlantean No. 110 on 10 April 1984 were somewhat unusual to say the least, as it was driven at a moderate speed into one of the roof stanchions inside the garage. It is seen in the bodyshop on 19 May 1984 and it didn't re-enter service until 12 July. Alongside is severe accident victim No. 124.

The last three Panthers in use by the Undertaking are seen inside No. 2 garage on 19 May 1984. Having been renumbered to 36/5/3 in October 1983, they were withdrawn at the end of August. The fleet then consisted of just eighty-three vehicles, the lowest total since 1945, and comprised seventy-nine Atlanteans, three Bristol midibuses and a solitary Olympian.

Service 34 had previously been the P4, but it ceased to be jointly operated after November 1980. Early morning, evening and Sunday journeys were operated via Brook Street as service 44. ELC-bodied Atlantean No. 128 looks quite appealing in this all-over advert colour scheme as it approaches the Ingol terminus in Barry Avenue on 27 October 1984.

From 2 January 1985 services 15 and 20 were altered to run via Sherwood Way to the junction of Eastway instead of turning at the Sharoe Green Lane circle. 1976-built ELC-bodied Atlantean No. 120 encounters some seasonal weather at the new terminus on 24 January 1985.

The last conventional Atlantean to enter the fleet was No. 177, which entered service on 1 July 1983. It was painted with this attractive all-over advert colour scheme in April 1985 and is seen in Larches Lane on 27 April, returning to town. This particular bus went on to carry two further advert schemes.

Atlanteans Nos 1 and 2 were used sparingly on ordinary stage carriage work as they were the preferred option for private hires and contract work, such as rail replacement services. However, on 17 May 1985 No. 2 has been allocated to work the 44 service from Ingol and is seen in Friargate, in the town centre.

There have only been three post-war years when no changes have been made to the fleet composition: 1973, 1985 and 1993. This was the scene in the dock shop on 18 May 1985, when Atlanteans Nos 127/48/50/66 were receiving attention. No. 127 was fresh out of the paint shop at the time.

In July 1985 a sewer collapse on Black Bull Lane caused severe disruption to service 22 for nearly four weeks. While the main service was diverted via Lytham Road and Garstang Road, an emergency service ran via Black Bull Lane using one of the Bristol midibuses, which was able to bypass the obstruction by traversing a series of narrower residential streets. The service ran as the 23 and No. 43 (renumbered from 343; originally being 243) is seen at Lytham Road roundabout on 13 July 1985.

When the Olympian demonstrator first joined the fleet it was given the number 3. It was renumbered to 33 in February 1985 and finally settled down to working on town services from April. It is seen departing the Sherwood terminus on 28 September 1985.

The Moor Nook service had its origins in the service to Moorside, which commenced running on 10 July 1939 and went as far as Ullswater Road. The service was partially extended along Pope Lane from 30 August 1948 and was firmly established as the MN from 8 March 1952. It became the 7 with the 1980 changes, but was then renumbered to 8 from 21 October 1985. Alexander-bodied Atlantean No. 142 is seen at the top of Pope Lane on 4 January 1986.

Deregulation of bus services took place on 26 October 1986, but few significant changes took place until the following year. However, one alteration that was implemented on 3 November 1986 was the extension of services 11 and 16 beyond the bus station, with alternate buses on each route running through to the railway station on Saturdays only. This arrangement continued until 11 July 1987, when they reverted back to their original routes. Showing service 111, ELC-bodied Atlantean No. 176 is seen alongside the railway station on 13 June 1987, having worked through from Ribbleton.

In April 1987 United Transport (t/a Zippy) commenced operations in the town with a fleet of minibuses, which eventually grew to comprise seventy-five vehicles. Zippy buses initially commenced running to Brookfield, Larches and Lea. At the same time, Preston Bus took delivery of a fleet of twenty Northern Counties-bodied Dodge minibuses, initially using them on services to Larches (27), Savick (30) and the Royal Preston Hospital (19), which all commenced on 21 April (the services actually ran the day before without collecting fares). No. 55 is seen in Blackpool Road at Ashton on 17 June 1987.

From 18 August 1986, certain journeys on services 15 and 20 were extended beyond Sherwood to the recently opened Fulwood Asda. These ran with service numbers 115 and 120. 1981-built ELC-bodied Atlantean No. 156 is seen at the Asda terminus on 19 June 1987.

From the same date, a series of 'free' bus services were provided by Asda to bring shoppers from various areas of the town and outlying areas. In total there were five such services, but three of them, from Garstang (D), Longridge (E) and Wesham (C), only ran on a Friday. 1982-built ELC-bodied Atlantean No. 165 is seen at Asda with a service A departure for Lea on 19 June 1987. This service had six round trips from Tuesday to Friday only, while service B from the Rose Bud also had six round trips but ran from Monday to Saturday. The services continued operating until 30 November 1990. No. 156 is seen behind on service 120.

The minibus service to Larches was hastily arranged, and for a short period it ran alongside the original service, which continued to operate using 'big' buses. The Zippy services to Larches (B) and Lea (C) commenced running on 20 April 1987, as did the Preston minibus service (with fare collection from the following day). Buses ran at frequent intervals and operated on the 'hail & ride' principle on certain sections of the route. Northern Counties-bodied Dodge No. 61 and Zippy Robin Hood-bodied Iveco Daily No. 053 are seen together at the Larches terminus on 21 June 1987.

The Zippy services expanded at an alarming rate, with services to Cadley (D) and Tanterton (H) starting in June. On 2 July 1987, Carlyle-bodied Freight Rover Sherpa No. 039 picks up in Harris Street on the Tanterton service, which competed directly with Preston's service 33. ELC-bodied Atlantean No. 131 waits behind on the service to Lea.

In August 1986 a significant number of school contract services were won on tender. Consequently, four Leyland Nationals were hastily acquired from the Merseyside PTE, principally to cover some of the school duties. Inevitably, they occasionally strayed onto ordinary services, and No. 7 is seen in Harris Street on the Lea service on 3 July 1987.

Service 19 was a completely new route, which commenced running on 21 April 1987 and ran via Deepdale Road, Watling Street Road and Sharoe Green Lane to the Broadwood Drive estate before terminating inside the hospital grounds. The last two of the initial batch of twenty Dodge minibuses had the slimmer style of body and were equipped with manual gears so they could be used for training purposes. No. 69 passes the Sharoe Green Lane turning circle on 4 July 1987.

In 1987 the operator was registered as Preston Borough Transport Ltd and adopted the fleet name of Preston Bus (minibuses carried Preston Mini fleet names). Preston Bus invested in this Duple-bodied Leyland Tiger coach with appropriate 'Preston Coach' fleet names. It was mainly used on advertised tours and excursions. Originally No. 40 in the fleet, it was later re-registered to PRN 909 and renumbered to 309. It is seen in the dock shop on 5 July.

For over two years from April 1987 the competition in Preston was extremely fierce. Minibuses from four other operators could be regularly seen in the town: Blackburn Transport, Fylde Transport, Ribble and United Transport (Zippy). Zippy Carlyle-bodied Sherpa No. 022 and Ribble Dormobile-bodied Sherpa No. 574 are seen together at the bus station on 11 July 1987.

In the years before and after deregulation, the operator Citibus of Chadderton was active in the Greater Manchester area. Nearly half of Preston's Panthers passed to this operator, usually third hand, including all but one (No. 228) of the Seddon-bodied examples. Former Nos 216/23 are seen at Piccadilly bus station in Manchester on 20 July 1987.

Services 5, 6 and 7 to Brookfield and Fulwood Row were renumbered from 35/6/7 in November 1985. The 5 and 6 were both withdrawn from 13 July 1987 while the 7 was converted to minibus operation at the same time. The 6 was reinstated a few months later, also using minibuses. Virtually brand-new Northern Counties-bodied Dodge No. 73 is seen in Watling Street Road on 21 July 1987. Despite having a design life of no more than five years, this bus was among the last of the type to operate with Preston and was not withdrawn until December 2001.

Minibus service 30 commenced operation on 21 April 1987 and ran to a different route to the previous Savick service, which ceased operation after the 18th, and which had largely employed the Bristol midibuses. Meanwhile, the Zippy operations were not just confined to the town environs, and service N to Lostock Hall was one of four out-of-town services introduced by United Transport on 20 June that primarily competed with Ribble. Northern Counties-bodied Dodge No. 62 is seen with Zippy three-axle Talbot Pullman No. 070 in Fishergate on 22 July 1987.

Preston Bus operated thirty-one of these early-style predominantly twenty-two-seat Dodge minibuses, with all but the last three entering service in a three-month period. Nos 67/70/1 were originally fitted with twenty high-backed seats while No. 44 had twenty ordinary bus seats but was equipped with extra luggage space for use on dedicated shoppers service 24. This service was introduced on 17 August 1987 using just the one bus. It survived until 9 October, after which it was withdrawn. The usual incumbent, No. 44, is seen in Black Bull Lane on 31 August.

The first of the restyled and rebadged twenty-five-seat Renault minibuses arrived in February 1988. Nineteen of the type entered service during that year, with a final two coming in April 1989. Nos 47–9 and 75–7 initially had the large 'PRESTON' outline on the bonnet, while the remainder were badged as 'Preston Mini'. Nos 49 and 85 are seen resting inside No. 2 garage on 14 May 1988, with the latter not entering service until two days later.

The year 1988 was probably when competition in Preston was at its height. Blackpool Transport Services had commenced operation of a number of services from Blackpool (185), Fleetwood (180/2) and Lytham (165), which worked into Preston. In retaliation, Preston Bus (in collaboration with Lancaster City Transport) commenced operation of service 39 on 16 July. The service ran seven days a week using Atlanteans from the Nos 141–50 batch on Monday to Saturday and minibuses on Sunday. Alexander-bodied Atlantean No. 146 is seen in Blackpool Road at Ashton on 13 August.

The Leyland Nationals were eventually repainted into the blue and ivory fleet colours, two years after their acquisition from Merseyside PTE. Northern Counties-bodied Renaults Nos 49 and 85 are sandwiched between recently repainted Nationals Nos 5 and 8 in the garage yard on 28 August 1988. No. 6 was written off in an accident in July 1987, while the other three were all withdrawn on 9 November 1989.

Alexander-bodied Atlanteans Nos 141–50 were specially fitted with cash trays for use on service 39 to enable the driver to give change. No. 144 is seen near Blackpool North station on its return journey to Preston on 29 August 1988.

Service 5 (previously 35) ran via Ribbleton Avenue and Cromwell Road to Brookfield. It was withdrawn in July 1987 and then reinstated in April 1988 using minibuses, with the route being extended beyond the Watling Street Road turning circle into the estate. Northern Counties-bodied Dodge No. 43 is seen at the new Oakworth Avenue terminus on 10 September 1988.

Over the years Preston Bus and its predecessors trialled a considerable number of demonstrator buses. For one week in October 1988, this fifty-one-seat Alexander-bodied Scania, which was painted in the colours of Derby City Transport, could be regularly seen on the Ribbleton service. It is seen here in Longridge Road on 21 October. This service was the usual test bed for demonstrators.

Service 21 lost its evening and Sunday service in June 1983. Later, the Sunday service was reinstated after deregulation day, and was then converted to minibus operation on that day of the week only from 19 July 1987. The Sunday service was again withdrawn in October, while the Monday to Saturday service was converted to minibus operation from 11 April 1988, with a change of route that saw buses looped via South Meadow Lane and Broadgate. Northern Counties-bodied Dodge No. 55 is seen in South Meadow Lane on 22 October 1988.

Leyland National No. 8 sparkles in the sunlight following its recent repaint. Along with Nos 5–7, this bus had been ordered by Southport Corporation, but entered service with the Merseyside PTE on 1 April 1974. It is seen in the garage yard on 22 October 1988.

Between 19 November and 24 December 1988, a Park & Ride service was operated on Saturdays only that ran from what was then the Polytechnic (now UCLAN) car park in Adelphi Street and then around the main town centre shopping streets. Two buses at a time were employed on the service, one of which was usually hired from Lancaster City Transport. Northern Counties-bodied Renault No. 89 waits for shoppers at the car park on 10 December 1988.

After a gap of five years, the Undertaking finally bought some new big buses for stage carriage work. The Lynx had been introduced by Leyland in 1986 to replace the National and four of the type entered the fleet in 1989. The first to arrive was No. 10, which is seen in the body shop on the day of its delivery, 18 March. Service 126 was an infrequent service that operated between 16 May 1988 and 13 October 1989, but it ran to Clayton Green and not Bolton.

The first batch of Leyland Lynx consisted of just four vehicles: Nos 10–3. No. 11 entered service on 22 March 1989 and is seen nine days later in Longridge Road at Ribbleton. This particular bus remained in service until September 2006, after which it was shipped to Malta, where it eked out several more years of service.

Service 43 has had several incarnations over the years. Renumbered from P6 in November 1980, it remained the last (on paper) jointly operated service until bus deregulation. It was converted to minibus operation on 11 April 1988, but at the same time it adopted an almost completely different route. Northern Counties-bodied Dodge No. 43 is seen in Cadley Causeway, one of the few roads that the new route had in common with the old 43, on 8 April 1989.

Service 23 was created on 13 July 1987 when alternate buses on service 22 were extended from Sharoe Green Lane via Sherwood Way and Eastway to the new Fulwood Asda store. At that time the store did not open on Sundays (not until 1994) and buses only ran as far as the junction of Sherwood Way and Eastway displaying the service number 123. Only a few weeks old, Lynx No. 13 waits at the Sherwood terminus on 23 April 1989.

Preston Bus didn't receive its second Olympian until March 1989, some five years after the acquisition of No. 3. Originally numbered 32, this Northern Counties-bodied example unusually had the number blind on the nearside. It is seen crossing the WCML in Eldon Street on 4 June 1989. It was later renumbered to 100 and was the first Olympian to be withdrawn in May 2008.

The Moor Nook service had been renumbered from 7 to 8 in October 1985. It was converted to minibus operation from 13 July 1987 with a change of route around the estate. No. 92 was the last new Renault minibus to enter service on 11 May 1989. It is seen on 4 June in Church Street.

Services had been using Brook Street for many years without any problems, despite the tight right-angled junction at Eldon Street. However, from 13 July 1987 it was decided to reroute inbound buses on the 33 and 44 via the parallel Plungington Road/Adelphi Street. This essentially just created a plethora of buses on the latter thoroughfare as it was already adequately served by the 22/3. Atlantean No. 157, with the rounded corners, contrasts with No. 122, which has stopped to pick up passengers in Adelphi Street on 17 June 1989. Brook Street regained an inbound service with the 43 in April 1988, and additionally with the new 31 to Savick in October 1989.

An additional service commenced running to Lea from 5 December 1988. Running to a basic hourly timetable from Monday to Saturday, the new service 24 was operated by minibuses and followed the same route as the 25 until it deviated around Thorntrees Avenue and Hawthorn Crescent before terminating at Aldfield Avenue. Northern Counties-bodied Dodge No. 61 is seen in Thornpark Drive at Lea on 4 July 1989.

Seen the same day in Whittle Hill at Woodplumpton, ELC-bodied Atlantean No. 112 is on the infrequent service 31 to Woodplumpton village. This service commenced running on 9 November 1987 and ran from Monday to Friday only. The route was partially circular, with buses running anti-clockwise from Fulwood via Broughton, Woodplumpton, Nog Tow and Tanterton, and then back to Fulwood. Atlanteans Nos 111–3 were usually employed as these were the only buses fitted with the blind inserts (although No. 131 later acquired a blind from one of these buses).

In March 1988 the Zippy operations were taken over by Ribble, who themselves were acquired by Stagecoach just over a year later. However, Ribble continued to operate most of the former Zippy routes so Preston Bus retaliated by starting a number of minibus routes in competition to the out-of-town Zippy routes. Services 4 to Penwortham and 17 to Bamber Bridge both started running on 16 May 1988 and were usually operated by the Renault minibuses. No. 77 is seen in Kingsfold Drive at Penwortham on 4 July 1989.

The Leyland Tiger coach saw a fair amount of usage, particularly during the summer months. No. 40 is seen at Skipton coach park, taking a breather while working a day trip to York on Friday 18 August 1989. It was replaced in March 2003, after sixteen years of service, by a second-hand Volvo B10M.

The first Atlanteans to be withdrawn were Nos 102–7 in July 1987, which were eagerly snapped up by the fledgling operator North Western Road Car Co. They were a common sight at Manchester's Piccadilly bus station for a number of years. Former No. 102 is seen alongside a Ribble Bee Line Sherpa in Wythenshawe bus station on 19 August 1989. The Atlantean is believed to still be in existence, being the subject of a long-term restoration project.

A third out-of-town minibus service was started on 15 May 1989, which ran to Longton. However, this was somewhat short-lived as Stagecoach Ribble and Preston Bus finally reached an agreement to reduce the competition and concentrate on their original areas of operation. Northern Counties-bodied Renault No. 82 is seen in Liverpool Old Road at Longton on 2 September 1989, two weeks before the service was withdrawn.

Metro-Cammell-bodied Leyland PD3/4s Nos 17/9 were converted to driver training buses in 1980 and were renumbered to T1 and T2. The latter was withdrawn and sold in January 1984, but the former lasted some ten years longer. T1 was renumbered to 99 in October 1983. It is seen in No. 3 garage on 11 November 1989. The bus was re-registered to PFF 997 before being sold in November 1994 and its 'PRN 909' registration was transferred to the coach. Having also been used on the Volvo coach, it was at the time of writing carried by Rotala Diamond North West Scania No. 30910.

A further batch of five Lynx were placed into service in November 1989. No. 14 is seen crossing the Lancaster Canal in Woodplumpton Road, returning from Tanterton on 7 January 1990. Following close behind is Blackpool Transport Leyland National No. 144 on service 182 from Poulton-le-Fylde.

Minibus service 114 was introduced on 11 May 1987 and ran as per the 14 to Holme Slack, but then continued on via Ronaldsway and Lambert Road to Munro Crescent. From July it replaced service 14 in the evening and on Sundays. Following a route alteration via Romford Road in November 1987, it was further altered to serve Hamilton Road from 22 January 1990. Dodge No. 62 is seen in Hamilton Road a week after this latest alteration.

Service 123 to Sherwood operated early mornings, late evenings and on Sundays, with the route being covered by service 23 at other times of the week. Another of the latest batch of Lynx, No. 17 is seen in Adelphi Street on Sunday 28 January 1990. The 123 number continued in use until May 2001, from when all but one early morning journey ran through to Asda.

Northern Counties-bodied Olympian No. 32 is seen again working on what should be service 123 from Sherwood. The number blind has now been repositioned on the offside. This view was taken in Adelphi Street on 28 January 1990.

Service 31 to Savick was an additional route to the estate. It was introduced on 16 October 1989 and operated via Brook Street and Inkerman Street to Ashton Lane Ends before continuing as service 30 from Cottam Lane. From August 1990 it was altered on Sundays to run via Fylde Road and the Docks, as per service 30. Northern Counties-bodied Renault No. 88 is seen in Friargate on 28 January 1990. No. 88 was one of a batch of three Renaults that entered service in November 1989.

This was a chance picture as it was not usual practice to line up similar types of buses in this fashion. Lynx Nos 11, 17, 10, 13 and 16 are seen together in the garage yard on Sunday 18 March 1990. The brick building behind is No. 3 garage, while No. 4 garage is alongside. This plot was used for the minibus compound that was constructed not long after this picture was taken.

The first production batch of Olympians to be received by Preston Bus was Leyland Workington-bodied Nos 34–7 in March 1990. Nos 34/5 were fitted out with seventy-two high-backed seats, whereas Nos 36/7 had seventy-eight ordinary bus seats. Service 35 to Tanterton was introduced on 16 October 1989 and operated via Fylde Road. It was interworked with service 33 and ran on Monday to Saturday, but not in the evenings. No. 34 is seen in Tanterton Hall Road on 14 April 1990.

Lynx No. 15 is seen in Ribbleton Lane on 28 April 1990. Other than Nos 10/1, all of the Lynx were fitted with high-backed seats. No. 15, later renumbered 215, entered service on 10 November 1989 and continued in service (other than a period in store under Stagecoach ownership) until 9 February 2016, during which time it attained celebrity status with Preston Bus and its subsequent owners, Rotala. It was sold to Morton's Travel of Tadley in December 2016 and is now semi-preserved.

A second service to Moor Nook commenced running on 16 October 1989 and it followed the route of the old Grange midibus service as far as Pope Lane before looping around the estate via Grizedale Crescent. There were a number of early morning and Sunday journeys that ran via Farringdon Park under the service number 109. Renault No. 87 is seen in New Hall Lane on 20 January 1990. This service was still operated by Stagecoach in 2018.

ELC-bodied Atlanteans Nos 1 and 2 were repainted into the standard livery in the summer of 1990. The high-backed seats were replaced by ordinary bus seats in June 1994 and they were renumbered to 181/2, though No. 182 was subsequently further renumbered to 180. No. 2 is seen in Tag Lane on 2 August 1990, just a couple of weeks after being repainted.

In February 1990 a protracted programme commenced to remove the centre exit doors from Atlanteans Nos 141–77. The first to be done was No. 154, and the programme was concluded with No. 152 in June 1993. 1982 example No. 171 is seen at the front of the depot on 11 August 1990, a couple of months after its conversion. Four additional seats were placed on the lower deck, raising the seating capacity to eighty-six.

Atlanteans Nos 1 and 2 were not the only buses to lose their three-blue-band livery as Olympian No. 33 was also repainted into the standard livery. It is seen leaving the bus station on 9 September 1990. The seventy-four high-backed seats were replaced by seventy-two ordinary bus seats (with additional luggage space) in October 1993 and it was renumbered to 133 in March 1995.

A third batch of Lynx, comprising six vehicles, entered service between November 1990 and January 1991, bringing the total operating to fifteen. The first of the batch was No. 23, which is seen in Tag Lane at Ingol on 12 January 1991. For some peculiar reason there was no No. 25.

Service 184 was originally a Ribble commercial service that ran from Preston to Salwick and served the Springfields nuclear fuel production installation. Following Ribble's withdrawal from the service, the contract was put out to tender, being subsequently operated by Preston Bus from 18 July 1988 until 25 October 1991. Renault No. 90 is seen in Tag Lane on 12 January 1991 heading for Preston bus station.

Another operator that found favour with former Preston Atlanteans was Sheffield Omnibus, which was based in the Sheffield District of Ecclesfield. The operator was so enamoured with the buses that they eventually bought twenty-four Atlanteans and based their livery on the Preston colours. Acquired in December 1990, former Preston No. 119 is seen at the Sheffield garage on 5 March 1991.

Following the sale of Alexander-bodied Atlanteans Nos 102–7 to North Western in September 1987, the next Atlanteans to be disposed of were Nos 101/8–10 to Hyndburn Borough Transport, which took place in November 1990. The four buses had their centre doors removed before entering service with Hyndburn. Now painted in the latter's attractive red and blue livery, the former No. 110 is seen in Accrington bus station on 16 March 1991.

Preston Bus took over the Port Way Park & Ride service from Stagecoach Ribble on 28 January 1991 and operated the service under contract to Lancashire County Council until 2 March 2013 (excepting the period of acquisition by Stagecoach), when the service was revised and linked with the Park & Ride service to Walton-le-Dale. PB initially used four second-hand Dodge minibuses. Former Cumberland MS Reeve Burgess-bodied No. 7 is seen leaving the Port Way site on 22 March 1991.

Preston Buses Before and After Deregulation

Following the introduction of more Lynx at the turn of the year, the operator reverted to buying double-deckers for their next new buses. These comprised four Northern Counties-bodied Olympians, which entered service in April 1991. Two days after entering service, on 13 April 1991, No. 104 is seen in Ribbleton Lane.

A number of Olympians were adorned with all-over advert schemes, but the fronts remained in fleet livery. The double crests on the front were only applied to a handful of buses. This particular advert is proclaiming the soon to be enacted 1992 Preston Guild. Leyland-bodied No. 35 is seen in Pittman Way, nearing the Asda terminus, on 6 May 1991.

The two Northern Counties-bodied Dodge S46 minibuses, Nos 68/9, are seen parked in 'the cage' at the depot on 19 May 1991. 'The cage' was a fenced compound that could hold around a dozen minibuses. Along with the Park & Ride buses, these were the first two Dodges to be disposed of in December 1994 following the acquisition of the first Metroriders.

Besides the ex-Cumberland Dodge, three more of the type, with the somewhat angular ELC-built bodies, were acquired from Magicbus/Stagecoach, which had originated from Barrow Borough Transport. Each of the trio was initially painted differently, although they did all eventually receive fleet livery. Nos 6 and 8 are seen waiting at the Port Way Park & Ride site on 5 July 1991.

The use of minibuses enabled roads to be served that had previously never seen a bus route. When the Marsh Lane dual carriageway was constructed, service 27 had to take a different route on its outbound journey, and instead of using Wellfield Road, it was diverted via Leighton Street and Pedder Street. Dodge No. 64 is seen climbing Leighton Street on 5 July 1991, just four days after the deviation was introduced.

Another of the Northern Counties quartet, No. 103, is seen in Tanterton Hall Road on 3 September 1991 while returning to the bus station. Service 32 was renumbered from 28 in July 1987. The other three of this batch of buses met an ignominious end in April 2017, when they were subject to a wanton act of vandalism that resulted in them being written off and sold for scrap.

ELC-bodied Atlantean No. 153 is seen in Pittman Way, close to the Fulwood Asda terminus, on 3 September 1991. At this time services 22 and 23 each ran to a ten-minute interval timetable, which resulted in a frequent five-minute service as far as Sharoe Green Lane. Substantial development work has since taken place in this area.

Alexander-bodied Atlantean No. 146 is seen in Tanterton Hall Road on 3 September 1991, just a few months after the centre doors were removed. The Alexanders also received four extra seats on the lower deck, but had one fewer on the upper deck, making them eighty-five seaters. No. 146 was sold to Lincolnshire Roadcar in November 1995, five years before any more of the batch were withdrawn.

Preston Bus ordered another eight Olympians for delivery in early 1992. However, No. 107 arrived on 12 October 1991 embellished with special 'Guild 92' lettering and was displayed at the Bus & Coach Exhibition at the Birmingham NEC two days later. It then returned to the Workington factory before entering service on 5 February 1992. It is seen in the body shop, among newly prefabricated bus shelters, on the day of delivery.

Alexander-bodied Atlantean No. 149 waits at the traffic signals at the junction of Friargate and Ring Way on 9 April 1992. From 13 January 1991 the upper part of Friargate was closed to all vehicles, so the bus would be required to turn left for the bus station. Blackpool Transport Optare Delta No. 113 is seen waiting behind.

Northern Counties-bodied Olympian No. 102 enters the bus station on 20 May 1992 following a trip to Fulwood. The elevated car park levels used to provide an excellent vantage point for a different approach to bus photography at the bus station.

Rather than return buses to the depot after the morning peak service, several buses could usually be found along the back wall by mid-morning. In this view taken on 20 May 1992, the line-up comprises ON No. 112, ANs Nos 177 and 146, ON No. 107 (Guild Bus) and ANs Nos 168 and 171. By this time the Atlantean door conversion programme was close to completion and all four Atlanteans in this view have received the modification.

The 'big bus' routes were not entirely restricted to vehicle types and both single- and double-deck buses would be used on the same route. 1989-built Lynx No. 12 is seen in Skeffington Road on 25 May 1992, returning from Holme Slack. Seen in the distance is the old Pavilion Stand, which stood on the east side of Preston North End's football ground and was demolished in 2007, being replaced by the new Invincibles' Stand.

The 1992 intake of eight Olympians included No. 106, which was new in 1991 and was first used as a demonstrator by Leyland Vehicles before entering service with Preston Bus on 2 April. It is seen in Lightfoot Lane on 13 June 1992 while returning to the bus station.

One of the earlier pictures in the book portrays Leyland PD3A/1 No. 90 in Cairnsmore Avenue in 1980. The thoroughfare is again the location for another picture of a bus on service 16, with only the lamp standards having changed in the intervening twelve years. 1990-built Lynx No. 24 is about to turn into Tudor Avenue as it nears the Farringdon Park terminus on 13 June 1992 as it nears the Farrington Park terminus.

An early morning picture taken the day before midsummer's day in 1992 sees a host of minibuses waiting to go out on the day's rosters. The line-up comprises Dodge Nos 54, 67, 70 and Renault No. 47. No. 54 was one of two Dodges that were renumbered just one month before their withdrawal in December 2001, becoming No. 540. Meanwhile, Nos 67 and 70 were both fitted with twenty high-backed seats as opposed to the more common twenty-two ordinary bus seats.

The changing face of the bus fleet is depicted in this view, which shows three of the Workington-built Olympians (Nos 36, 110/4) at rest at the front of No. 2 garage on 4 July 1992. The latest additions had replaced Atlanteans Nos 131–40, which all went to Sheffield Omnibus. Other than the previously mentioned No. 146, no more of the type were withdrawn for the next five years as the company concentrated on replacing the first generation of minibuses.

In 1991 the size of the fleet had reached its maximum ever total of 132 vehicles. However, in 1992 it comprised 129 vehicles, consisting of thirty-nine Atlanteans, fifteen Lynx, fifty-six minibuses, eighteen Olympians and the Leyland Tiger coach. In addition, five buses were used on loan, three of which joined the fleet for Guild Week, again raising the total to 132. Earlier in the year, on 25 July 1992, Merseybus-liveried Northern Counties-bodied Dennis Lance J215 OCW is seen in Ribbleton Lane on the usual recipient service for demonstrators.

Olympian No. 113 is seen in Sherwood Way on the Sunday variant of service 23 on 23 August 1992. With the expansion of the route network, additional bus shelters were required. These were generally bespoke, being ordered and paid for by the council but manufactured in-house in the depot body shop and assembled on site.

1992 was a 'Preston Guild' year – an event that takes place once every twenty years. During what is known as Guild Week, which is usually the first week in September, several large processions take place, which bring the town to a halt. On procession days the railway station forecourt was used as a small temporary bus station and Dodge minibuses Nos 57 and 54 are seen parked up on 31 August 1992. Services to Larches and Lea were provided from this location.

One of the most unusual buses ever to work for the Undertaking was this ELC-bodied Atlantean. New to Blackburn Borough Transport in September 1972, it later passed to City of Lancaster and was converted to open-top format. It was hired by Preston Bus for the duration of Guild Week and was used in ordinary passenger service on the Farringdon Park and Tanterton routes. CoL No. 84 is seen in Tag Lane at Ingol on 1 September 1992 while being pursued by Renault No. 77 on service 44.

In addition to the Port Way Park & Ride service, six additional services were operated by PB and Stagecoach to temporary sites around the town. 'Guild Bus' Olympian No. 107 is seen heading for the Esplanade at Frenchwood on 1 September 1992 on special service 39. Of the eight Olympians received that year, Nos 107/14 were fitted out with seventy-two high-backed seats, whereas the other six had seventy-eight ordinary bus seats.

This was the scene at the bus station during one of the processions on the afternoon of 3 September 1992. As many of the town centre streets were closed, only a limited service could be provided, and several routes were suspended for the duration of the procession. Consequently, most of the buses on view are static. To the fore is Olympian No. 32, however, which is unusually being employed on minibus service 9 to Moor Nook.

Normally operated by minibuses, the Port Way Park & Ride service was turned over to double-deckers for Guild Week. Alexander-bodied Atlantean No. 141 is seen waiting for custom at a fairly deserted Port Way site on 3 September 1992.

Despite the display on the blind, ELC-bodied Atlantean No. 163 is actually working the Park & Ride service to Port Way, but due to road closures it has been diverted to start at the railway station instead of Lune Street. Behind is Dodge No. 73 and on-loan Metrorider demonstrator J363 BNW. This view was captured on 3 September 1992.

Several Guild events were staged on Avenham Park and required the transportation of schoolchildren to the venue. Northern Counties-bodied Olympians Nos 102/3 and ELC-bodied Atlantean No. 173 have been assisted by on-loan Rossendale Transport 1987-built ELC-bodied Olympian No. 88. The quartet is seen waiting in Broadgate on 3 September 1992 before transporting the children back to school.

One of the highlights of Guild Week is the Trades Procession, which, as the name suggests, is the opportunity for local businesses and organisations to promote their services. Previous Guilds in the twentieth century had attracted a large number of entries and massive crowds to this event. Though the purse strings were somewhat tighter in 1992, it was still a huge event. Entry number 165 was Northern Counties-bodied Renault No. 85, which was sponsored by Derian House Children's Hospice. It is seen here wending its way up Corporation Street on 3 September 1992.

Following its acquisition in January 1991, ELC-bodied Dodge No. 6 was repainted out of its Stagecoach colours into all-over white, which was intended as the base for an advert scheme. However, the advert never materialised and it was eventually painted into the fleet colours with somewhat crude Park & Ride lettering. It is seen at Port Way on 28 November 1992, just a few days after emerging from the paint shop.

The solitary Eastern Coach Works-bodied Olympian No. 33 is seen alongside 'the cage' in the depot yard on 16 January 1993. This bus remained in service until May 2009. By then in the ownership of Stagecoach, it was placed in store until March 2010 (pending the outcome of the Competition Commission's report), when it was sold to a preservation group.

ELC-bodied Atlanteans Nos 113/6/7/20 were sold to Warrington Borough Transport in November 1990. The centre exit doors were removed by S. & T. Coachpainters Ltd of Blackburn before they entered service with Warrington. The former No. 113 is seen at the Wilderspool depot on 7 March 1993 in the company of ELC-bodied Bristol RE No. 71. Somewhat confusingly, they were given fleet numbers 111–4 and were eventually repainted into red and white.

From 1 April 1993 the company ceased to be council owned and was the subject of a management and employee buyout. The operator was henceforth registered as 'Preston Transport Holdings Limited', but continued to trade as Preston Bus. This chance picture, taken on 17 April 1993, sees a line-up of five of the 1980-built Alexander-bodied Atlanteans, with Nos 149/8/7/6/1 laying over between duties.

This is another view of the same quintet, as seen from the car park levels, which has now been joined by No. 150 of the same batch. No. 150 is seen departing for Ribbleton Gamull Lane. Following their withdrawal from service in 2000/01, four of these buses saw further service with local operator J. Fishwick & Sons.

Preston Buses Before and After Deregulation

Northern Counties-bodied Olympian No. 104 was the only one of the quartet to carry an all-over advert livery. It is seen at the Holme Slack turning circle on 23 June 1993. The circle was commissioned on 17 April 1978 but fell out of use when service 14 was withdrawn in lieu of the 114 from 27 October 1997, thereafter only being used by a handful of school buses until it was brought back into use for the truncated service 14 in September 2018.

The first service to Ribbleton commenced running on 26 January 1905 and was operated by electric trams to the long since demolished Bowling Green Hotel, which was situated just short of this location. It was converted to motorbus operation in November 1933 and henceforth operated to Chatburn Road, which is on the left, just ahead of the Lynx. From 1 January 1948 it became the GL/P5, which then turned round at Gamull Lane. This subsequently became service 10, which was eventually replaced by the 11, which was routed through the Grange estate. Olympian No. 36, heading for town, passes Lynx No. 13 on 14 August 1993. Following the takeover by Rotala, the service was relinquished to Stagecoach on 25 January 2011, and was given the number 1A.

ELC-bodied Atlantean No. 161 entered service on 23 November 1981 and the centre doors were removed in December 1992. Still looking immaculate, it was captured in New Hall Lane on 14 August 1993, heading back to town. The slogan on the front reads 'Your Friendly Service' – one of four different messages that were applied to the Atlantean fleet not long after deregulation.

The final picture depicts Northern Counties-bodied Olympian No. 32 leaving the bus station on 18 November 1993. With the station having been opened on 12 October 1969, this scene was repeated day-in, day-out until 2017. After proposals to demolish the building were overturned and it was granted listed building status, a multi-million-pound refurbishment scheme has seen all bus services grouped on the opposite (east) side. The west side concourse still awaited redevelopment in 2018.